THE EXTRA YEAR

JORY POST

Jory Post

ANAPHORA LITERARY PRESS

QUANAH, TEXAS

ANAPHORA LITERARY PRESS
1108 W 3rd Street
Quanah, TX 79252
https://anaphoraliterary.com

Book design by Anna Faktorovich, Ph.D.

Printed in the United States of America, United Kingdom and in Australia on acid-free paper.

Author photo by: Jon Silver: http://migrantmedia.com
Cover photo by: Irene Reti Photography:
https://ireneretiphotography.smugmug.com/

Published in 2019 by Anaphora Literary Press

The Extra Year
Jory Post—1st edition.

Library of Congress Control Number: 2019911695

Library Cataloging Information

Post, Jory, 1950-, author.
    The extra year / Jory Post
    90 p. ; 9 in.
    ISBN 978-1-68114-508-2 (softcover : alk. paper)
    ISBN 978-1-68114-509-9 (hardcover : alk. paper)
    ISBN 978-1-68114-510-5 (e-book)
1. Poetry—Subjects & Themes—Death, Grief, Loss.
2. Poetry—Subjects & Themes—Places.
3. Health & Fitness—Diseases—Cancer.
PN6099-6110: Collections of general literature: Poetry
811: American poetry in English

CONTENTS

For Karen, who lights up my life

Cold

It turned cold early this year, a freeze that occupies my nose, slashes through my heart on the way to swollen ankles and numb toes. Karen puts electric blankets on the bed, my writing chair, buys Duraflame logs by the trunkload. She is my heat, brings warm breasts to rub this morning as I sit in our foot-of-the-bed writing studio. The shock of my iced hands on her skin causes a scream, a jump away from me. I wonder if I affect everyone this way? Do they see small icicles dangling from my eyebrows? Does the oncologist remain aloof because my nostrils shoot frigid streams of air? Has the large malignant tumor in my pancreas stolen my body temperature to encase itself in ice, refusing to allow a CT scan to show any reduction in size or vascular complication? There is so much I don't know about temperature, surviving a long winter, keeping the people around me warm and happy.

Smooth Dirt

When I was four I carried two metallic sifters into the garden each morning, set up school between the pumpkins and cabbage, a red plastic trowel still stuck in the ground from the day before. I'd dig and scoop soft clods into the first sifter, squeeze the handle and watch the silt flow into the tight screen of the second sifter. I'd turn the trowel upside down, use the handle to squeeze dirt through the second screen into little pyramids on the ground. With my bare hands I would slide my fingers through the mounds, lift and spread my smooth dirt, make pies and cakes and airports and tunnels until my hands were black, my fingernails full. It was much later in real school that my education solidified. I came to value the importance of clean nails. Using two sifters was redundant. Smooth dirt was a concept no one understood, so I stopped making it.

Lobbies

Always full. People waiting. For what's next. Good news and bad. Wearing compression socks and saris and Giants hats and Birkenstocks and loose-fitting clothes to give easy access to body parts. Filling out forms. Remembering what meds they're on. If their allergies have changed. Smiling and frowning. Happy to still be alive. Wishing they weren't. Bumping into acquaintances, friends. Talking with strangers. Comparing war stories. Wearing face masks. Bandaged arms. Collapsed veins. Tattoos that sag. Canes and walkers that drag. Rows of clinics with doctors on time, late, out. High blood pressure. Twitching eyes. Tapping of anxious feet. Crossword puzzles and magazines and way too many cell phones. Who knew a life could end up here. In a lobby. With a tribe of others. Waiting. Eye contact made between one with a bald head and another sitting in a wheelchair. A nod from each. Like the exchange of blood, finger to finger, forever linked.

Burn, Baby, Burn

When I was young, I didn't know who killed God or why. I didn't know how to interpret empty holes in the photograph albums. At age fifteen I brought a girlfriend, Kathy, home to meet my parents. I had never seen them so strange, quiet. I asked them later what was going on, and that's when I learned I had a sister who died of crib death, whose name was Kathy, who would have been the same age as the Kathy I had brought home. It was my aunt who told me twenty years later about the night it happened, about how my mom found her, about how my dad went through the house gathering everything related to Kathy, piled it on the front lawn, poured gasoline on it, and set it ablaze. "That's when God died, for all of us," Aunt Bev said. In my philosophy-of-religion class I learned otherwise. It was Friedrich Nietzsche who killed God nearly one hundred years earlier, long before Kathy died, before my dad lit the match.

Capture and Release

My wife's snoring—percussive inhaling, cello and bass on the exhale, an occasional hint of tuba—provides the orchestral accompaniment to a glorious entrance into an early-morning dream: Elizabeth Bishop, with her white-gloved hand perched inside the elbow crook of Mark Doty, allows him to deliver her to one red velvet chair in a large auditorium before he takes the stage, makes himself comfortable behind a podium, picks up a baton, and begins to fillet her poem "The Fish," reading from his book *The Art of Description*. Doty removes the bones she has so elegantly constructed, licks each one clean, polishes them, displays them for public viewing, before taking the time and care to reconstruct this masterpiece of nature, removing his fingerprints, his DNA, pretending nothing has happened. He returns to her seat, offers his arm, and they depart, an unearthly collaboration complete, as my wife's breathing returns to normal, and I pull myself from bed, hauling a large fish in a net to my writing desk, and attempt to capture it before the release.

Tiny Bones

For the third time today I'm walking the dog past the owl pellets baked on the sidewalk below the palm tree. This time I bend over and examine the tiny bones, think of the remains as the natural selection of predator and prey, rather than the carnage it really was. The dog sniffs the pile before spraying urine on it, claiming it as her own.

Katherine

Henry Kaiser is buried there. James Earp, the older brother of Wyatt. My great-grandparents, in the walls behind granite. My six-week-old sister is buried there. It took me sixty years to visit the Mountain View Cemetery nestled on 226 acres in the Oakland foothills. To drive through the gates. To look through the 1953 record book. To be given the number 247 and told to look in the children's cemetery behind the mausoleum. There was no gravestone 247. No engraving reading *Katherine Lorraine Post, Nov. 3, 1952 to Jan. 20, 1953*. A few weeks later they called. Said they found it. That all was in order now. I drove back, made my way over and through the graves of other children. I couldn't tell whether the concrete number and granite gravestone had been found in a dusty storage shed or recently chiseled new. It didn't matter. I was finally able to do something for my sister. When I was two, I threw my doll Mary in the fireplace. Nothing was in order now. It never will be. But I know where to find her, if I ever go back.

"P" Club

Our CPA has prostate cancer and Parkinson's disease. I have pancreatic cancer. Michelle's husband has polio. We're looking for others who might round out our "P" club: someone with psoriasis, pelvic inflammatory disease, pinkeye, pneumonia. We'll only meet at parks, and we'll eat pastries, pies, pizza, peanuts, pears, and passionfruit. We will piss and moan, procrastinate, prevaricate, and pontificate. When one of us is cured, or dies, we'll throw a party.

Lather

That we are imprisoned by our well-earned routines has never been a question. After I switched from a 1967 Camaro to a 2016 Prius, it took months to remember not to reach for a key. Sometimes, when driving down 30th Avenue, I'll make the wrong turn into an apartment complex I lived in my whole life. In the early-morning hours I might jolt awake drenched in sweat, having spent the night in the angry clenches of a former wife. Today, waking in a resort villa the likes of which I've never imagined, I step into the shower, focus my aging eyes on the bottles in the soap rack, and remove the lid from the shampoo in preparation for a nice lather, like I've done my whole life. Then I lift a palm full of thick liquid toward my head, only to be reminded that I haven't had a beard or hair since the ninth round of chemo. It makes me laugh out loud, and I lather my shiny scalp anyway.

Along for the Ride

The first time I saw the spider's web wrapped around my sideview mirror I took it personally. Wanted to grab the hose and wash it away. This is *my* car. I see things with that mirror, look at where I'm going when I back out. I sit in the driveway, observe the intricate design. The spider as survivor, as artist. How does it know where to intersect the strands of filament? To create the perfect amount of tautness to trap its prey? I see her head peek out from behind the mirror. Is she watching me, or checking for lunch? We drive away together. A day full of errands. To Staff of Life for #592 granola. To Attilia's Antique's Store to look for boxes. I skip the planned car wash. By the time we reach home, she's taken center stage in the web. Flaunting herself. Enjoying the ride. Is it a Zen thing that I've chosen to let her live? Is it really my choice?

Mining

My friend is home from Colombia. She wants to visit—which is good. Others can't or won't. They become tongue-tied, unable to find the words to describe to themselves how they feel, unable to imagine themselves in conversation with me. Finding mortality in my ashen face, my thinning hair, my shrinking body. Let them stay away. We have mining to do, healing to consider, observations to be made. A forced expansion that we willingly accept. We both have stories to tell in ways that are better than we've ever found before. She has been to Colombia, been smashed into by a huge truck, driven on roads that appear headed nowhere. I have stayed in Santa Cruz, sat in an infusion chair that often appears headed nowhere. What might we pry loose this time, what gems may tumble from our mouths, waiting to be polished?

Innocence

In the beginning, my left eye became blurry, light faded, and I lost my keys. On the second day, morning and evening merged into one thing, unnoticed by me in sleep, and the hair on the left side of my scalp thinned. On the third day, the earth of my skin began to dry and flake, the sea of my bladder began to release six times a night, and someone from Kuala Lumpur hijacked my Netflix account. On the fourth day, a fog covered the moon and a smog blocked the sun, and I became angry, temporarily lost my battle to remain calm. On the fifth day, a dove flew into the sliding-glass door, did not recover, and I thought more about death than I wanted to. On the sixth day, Hal Blaine, the drummer of the Wrecking Crew, died at age 90, and I couldn't recall the lyrics to "A Hazy Shade of Winter." On the seventh day, I refused to rest, needed to stay awake all night and try to recover something, anything, if never again my innocence.

Port

I have a port in my chest, buried beneath the skin, with a small plastic tube that runs up to my carotid artery and back down to the right atrium of my heart. The port makes life easier for the nurses who draw my blood and fill my veins with Abraxane and Gemzar every Wednesday. It seems a waste to access it so infrequently, so I've made my own use for the port: I bare my chest, lie flat on the bed, close my eyes, and plug into the universe, the accidental and intentional light shooting down into the port, through every cell in my body, cycling through and around my pancreas and lifting gently the tendrils wrapped around arteries and veins. I allow the doctors to temporarily lease my body, take control with their established protocols to shrink my tumor, but I retain my right to other methods, ones that fall outside their means.

44 Years

Eleven. Voices laughing and partying in the backyard, until they were drowned out by the wails of an ambulance that pulled into our driveway. A stretcher brought through the house, placed next to my dad who was on the lawn, his bloodied face and shirt narrowing my focus. They carried him away, drove him to Mt. Eden Hospital with my mom. My sister and I stayed home with neighbors given the strict policy of no visitors under twelve. He disappeared for nine months, the red vomiting unleashed by a bleeding ulcer, which in those days was chopped out along with three-fourths of his stomach, which in those days was accompanied by a lengthy staph infection, which in those days was accompanied by addiction to morphine. He died on Halloween 44 years later. When I think of these medical bookends of his life, I'm not sure which changed me more, waiting on the couch staring out the front window past a stand of naked birch trees for nine months, or holding his hands staring into his eyes seconds before he stopped breathing. No. It was definitely the eyes, angry and fearful, wondering what was going on, the day after his oncologist told him he'd live for two more years. I wore those eyes for six months.

Lists

Monday morning I compile a list of things I know nothing about: changing diapers, the theory of relativity, names of a few neighbors, how to use our Instant Pot, where exactly my mom stores my dad's ashes, the final 600 pages of *Infinite Jest* that I didn't finish, the life span of sand crabs, anything at all about how to play or read music, what causes the headache that begins behind my left eye and slices to the base of my neck. On Tuesday I start with the easy ones, use Google to discover that Emerita can live up to three years, that $E=mc^2$ shows that energy and mass are interchangeable. Wednesday, I open David Foster Wallace's tome to page 479 and read without food or bathroom breaks, fight my way through the footnotes, reach page 1,079 before dinner. Thursday afternoon I follow the mail truck around my cul-de-sac, look at letters and bills in boxes until I have all the neighbors' names memorized. That night I sleep on one pillow instead of two. My head feels slightly better when I wake at 4:30 a.m. on Friday. I know I'm running behind, know I'm ignoring the more difficult items. I spend the day on YouTube, learn about frets and staffs and clefs and chords and melody and how *every good boy does fine* and timing and meter, and by evening, my head aches. On Saturday morning I make the steel-cut oats in the Instant Pot with my wife's guidance. On Saturday afternoon I visit the neighbor with the two-year-old, spend too much time there, but just enough to see the little girl wriggle on the floor, ready for a change, which I observe. Sunday evening while playing pinochle at my mom's, I'm almost there, just need to walk down the hall, open the closet, and hunt. But the kryptonite stops me, turns me into a puddle. Tomorrow is another Monday, a new list. I'd like to start with a blank page, but I don't. I begin it with "Where exactly does my mom store my dad's ashes?"

Nhoj

My uncle Gene was the director and head psychologist at a minimum-security CYA camp called the Bar-O Ranch thirty-two miles above Crescent City, surrounded on all sides by the Smith River. The boys who lived there could easily walk up to the highway and leave if they wanted, but there was nowhere to go. One of the boys, John, had lived on a ranch with his family before he began stealing cars. When the new calf was born at the Bar-O, John became his caregiver. He named it Nhoj. Two years later, a few months short of John's release date, it was time for Nhoj to provide steaks and hamburger and roasts for the boys' dinners in the mess hall. The butcher from town would drive out in the morning and John would assist him. John's bunkmate told my uncle that he had slipped out of their room just after midnight and never came back. They found him five miles from the Oregon border sitting along the side of the road, a big grin on his face, Nhoj's collar in his lap. "At least one of us got out."

Revision

My friend said today that my writing will help me defeat this thing. Will it be these prose poems that twist themselves around my thoughts, find their way out of my restless brain daily? Or is it the dozens of short stories waiting to find their unexpected but obvious endings? No. It's the novel waiting for a final revision. The one where I have given Louise my cancer. The one where she has left town, refuses to sit down and write. Last seen, she was on a train heading across Canada. I have investigators tailing her now. This thing is not over until they bring her back, chain her to the chair.

Quilted

I watch the flowers on my mom's handmade quilt rise and fall as my wife's steady heart keeps us all alive. Asleep or awake, she avoids a-fib and arrhythmia. Like the steady hands of a Rolex watch, she keeps us attuned to planetary waves, to bodily functions and needs we might overlook. Little did Mom know when she selected the colorful materials and stitched patches together that the finished piece would be worn like a coat of armor, impenetrable and flexible, perfect for warriors like us.

Equal Value

When I was eight my neighbor had a large cardboard box that had once held a black-and-white RCA television but was now home to army tanks, military vehicles, infantrymen, and other paraphernalia for waging a significant make-believe war. I would pick first, and George would follow with something of equal value, until the box was empty, each of us surrounded by our props of destruction. When my first wife and I separated, I brought the cardboard boxes. She filled her first one with china and silver. I filled mine with used poetry books from my bookshelf. My second box was filled with tools from the workbench in the garage. Hers contained antiques and expensive wedding gifts we'd never used. We carried my filled boxes to the car and she laughed, said, "You have a pretty poor sense of equal value." I picked out the signed first edition of Jack Gilbert's *Views of Jeopardy* from my first box. "Have you read this?" I asked. She smirked, walked away, to begin the life she had been looking for.

Wailing

When I received the call this week about my uncle's death, I wailed and shook spiders from corners of the ceilings, the poor dog trying to hide her ears from my insanity. The second death came in through email. Kit from my improv writing group had passed a few days ago. My grieving quieter, more thoughtful than raw. At Nob Hill this morning I saw Lance and he shared that our friend Jane had died, Jane who was my pancreatic cancer companion. My grief for her was more personal. She blazed a pathway to my future. When I'm sinking, I go to the Internet, find numbers and data that soothe me. I discovered that 6,316 people die each hour, 151,600 each day, over 1 million every week. I spent the day trying to convince myself that my three friends were in good company, until I finally gave up, broke down and wailed for all 1 million.

Ice Hole

SETI has been searching for signs of intelligent life in the universe for decades. They send signals to distant planets in hope of recognition. Their work relies on patience, a faith rooted deeper than science or God. My friend who lives in Tahoe near Squaw Valley is buried in snow this winter, yet still carves out an ice hole and sends me an email seeking proof of life. I send her a quick reply, leave trails of breath between words, ease her discomfort while sharing that mine has kept me horizontal this week, out of touch. "I know," she says. "I just wanted to remind you that you're still breathing."

Role Model

There was a time I considered myself a role model: for students, their parents, my fellow teachers, my family and friends, anyone who'd listen and pay attention to what I had to share. I wrote books, presented ideas to teachers in their classrooms and at local and national conferences. I was pure, dedicated, driven in my quest for knowledge and truth. But something shifted, as if the tumblers in locks had magically been altered. It may have had something to do with the Loma Prieta earthquake and the loss of lives. It could have been the insanity of the Gulf wars. Or working for a corporate monster like Apple for eleven months. Or simply the rotation and replacement of brain cells. Thirty years later I can hear the brass tumblers realigning themselves. I may publish another book. This time it will be about what I don't know.

Theories

There is a one-minute span each morning between 4:00 and 5:00 when the cable box shuts down, the lights go out, time stops. Eventually the word "Boot" appears, some indecipherable letters and numbers, a bit of flashing, and finally the time reappears. It's only one minute out of 1,440 per day. But I worry about it. In general, I don't pay attention to conspiracy theories, think most theorists have had a screw or two misplaced. This one is different. Why would this worldwide corporation interrupt my sleep every morning every day of the year? Did they form a partnership with a sleep-apnea company, a worldwide ruse to sell more CPAP machines? Or are they invading our privacy in more subversive ways, uploading and downloading videos of our bedroom activities? I don't know what the truth is, but every morning I check my pillow for loose screws.

Pecking Order

Even though they're the smallest, the wrens have free rein, stay out of the way, don't eat much, have formed unspoken alliances with the others. The doves remain true to their cliché, peaceful, nonconfrontational, move out of the way as needed. The black-headed grosbeaks show up in numbers, take over for a few minutes until they've filled up and move on. It's the blue jays who start the squawking, noisy in flight, screaming off the others, even before they land on suet and hanging bags and trays full of seeds. They open their beaks and howl, call to their families to join them. Finally, the acorn woodpeckers roar in like kamikazes, sharp beaks flashing, take over for as long as they like, at least until the band-tailed pigeons arrive in size and quantity and set up house.

When I've left the birds at home, arrive at the infusion center, I take my place in the lobby. We are young and old, male and female, Hispanic and African-American, Christian and Muslim, frail and vibrant. Aliens have inhabited each of our bodies. We're not there to fight for food, establish a hierarchy. Okay, maybe with the hats. One wears a hand-knit wool cap her daughter made. Another wraps a silk scarf around in layers. Warriors beanies and Raiders hats, berets and furry things from Mongolia, and others walk in oblivious to cold and vanity and bare their hairless heads, proud.

Yoda

When I look in the mirror and find my hairless head and face, I see Yoda staring back at me, big ears extending sideways, a small but powerful presence, eager to train me in the way of the Jedi. I'd like to say yes, give myself over to him, let him instruct me in the pathway to unlocking the secrets of immortality. But the image morphs, becomes Walter White, a stern frown on his face, and he wants to take me down a different path, wants me to stay in my underwear all day long, wants me to cook meth in the desert, reminds me how our similar fates point elsewhere. I need to make a decision. Am I willing to live, like this, forever, or am I happy to die, let someone else take my place? If only it were that easy, to say this or that, to pretend the decision is really mine to make.

Exile

A long, warm, and wordless embrace is what usually preceded my friend Don and me sitting down at Little Shanghai for lunch. He'd remove his hat and backpack, slide out a journal and pen, and often begin the conversation with one word. On this day, the final time I saw him before a heart attack whisked him away, the word was *Exile*. He started with Napoleon's exiles to Elba and St. Helena. We went on so long with a list that included Imelda Marcos and Seneca and Casanova and Juan Perón, all of whom were removed by those in power, that we forgot to order lunch. Once the pot stickers and dan dan noodles arrived, we changed our tastes, switched to the Dalai Lama and Leon Trotsky and Roman Polanski and Pablo Neruda, all of whose exiles were somewhat self-imposed. During the green-tea ice cream I tossed out J.D. Salinger, which set off a half-hour debate about whether exiling oneself to a cabin on one's own property appropriately fit the definition of exile.

Since Don was banished from the planet in 2012, I have ignored an unfulfilled promise. I think about him always but have avoided our unwritten pact. When one of us, usually him, opened a one-word study, we would wrestle with it together until it was either wrung out or became transformed into one of his famous essays. Exile took itself and me with it to a remote island without people and words, and it's taken me six years to find my way home.

Almost Done

My wife has taken Pepper to the vet this morning. She is losing her hair, doesn't like her food, has growths on her skin, moves slowly after eighty-four dog years. I'm ordering a blueberry-banana smoothie with whey protein at New Leaf Market on 41ˢᵗ when the text comes in. "Pepper is almost done." I double over weeping. We've known her only a couple of years, but we've become close. She's ours. The second text follows after I've righted myself. "She's getting IV fluids, antibiotics, and going home with special food for her upset stomach." After twelve weeks of chemo I know how she feels. Will someone text me when I'm almost done?

Duraflame

There is more to the Duraflame-logs story than I first suspected. When Costco ran out, she went to Safeway. When Safeway ran out, she went to Nob Hill. Worried that Nob Hill would run out, she ordered them online and the boxes showed up on our doorstep. At first, I didn't understand. Why was she so obsessed with them? But then I remembered the 1996 Olympic Games in Atlanta, when Muhammad Ali lit the Olympic torch. Keeping a vigilance so the eternal flame would stay lit, staring into the hot eyes of death, saying, "I can beat you."

Polish

Some nights are full of molasses, all slow movement, reducing thoughts to a random cluster of letters. Words carved in granite are impossible to slide into place, awkward and clumsy, garbled when spoken as if stolen from someone else's dream. A single polished stone, pushed to the top of a mountain, the boulder of Sisyphus seeking balance, companionship, a perfect partnership. How can I spend another night like this, watching one digital number after another tick by, selecting a word, replacing it, waiting for an exact combination, climbing up and down the mountain, trying to create a sentence I have never written or seen before? How can I not?

Semantics

Farnaz slipped into my brain last night and got stuck there as I fell asleep. The results of the MRI had come back negative, so neither of us worried she'd fall into a pit of rapidly growing cells that could overwhelm. It was more about the lack of an exit strategy. She had come in for a reason that was not immediately clear to either of us. After hours of hunting through lobes, we understood she was there to give me a gift, one she had yet to discover, one which I wasn't sure I was ready to accept. In the occipital lobe, we donned miner's lamps, needed to see where we were going, looking for a vision of what we were seeking, aware of color differentiation and motion detection. We closed our eyes as we moved into the parietal lobe, used our hands to work our way through, touched everything, felt for changes in temperature, pain pockets. We opened our eyes in the frontal lobe, got stuck in dopamine neurons longer that we should have, looking for reward, attention, overcome by short-term memory tasks, planning, motivation. Finally, we reached the temporal lobe, where we came to understand the journey a little better, how it was all about long-term memory, the meaning we were seeking together, the processing of semantics. When I woke in the morning she was gone, had left me with this: "Everything ends with meaning." And I have no idea what this means.

Recognition

When I look in the mirror, I'm surprised at the head staring back at me. My once-thick hair used to cover my ears, which now stick out sideways. The beard I had worn for forty-six years was brown, thick, speckled with grey. Now a scraggly mustache tries to cling to my upper lip. I don't know why it shocks me to see similar reactions in others who haven't seen me since the transformation. Last week two friends in a booth at a restaurant. I pulled up an open chair and sat staring at them. Carl wasn't sure what to think. Was I just another homeless guy off Pacific Avenue who'd come in to harass them? I could see him start to work on my face, try to pull out something familiar, but it didn't work. I talked to him, told him that maybe the voice would eventually help. After a couple of minutes, he finally said, "Oh my god! Jory?" Now when I go out, I look for people I know, who used to know me. I look forward to the shock, look forward to telling them my name, to see if they remember who I used to be.

Snail's Pace

At Cordevalle Resort for three days and nights of R & R, my body forgets how to react to immersion in a hot tub. I sit on the edge of the bed after, urging my newly found vertigo to stay away. Outside the slider the sand traps and fairways spread across the expansive valley like a scene out of the Civil War. Armored vehicles on the move, clubs swinging, objects flying. Outside the window, a snail has climbed onto a four-foot mat and begins a journey. Maybe I should get down on the hardwood floors of our villa, inch myself forward from the bedroom to the front door, stretch the length of my own journey, look for spiders under the bed, observe everything in detail from this new perspective, a kind of Jimi Hendrix—*I want to hear and see everything*. I touch the front door with my nose, inch back toward the bedroom, find curled sow bugs in a corner, a crumpled Kleenex under a chair, before I reach the slider, where the snail is only halfway across the mat. Too fast, I need more time on the floor, use only fingertips. So much more to see, trails of dust like tiny racetracks used by small creatures in the middle of the night, the fine handiwork of carpenters along baseboards, a view of the ceiling I never could have imagined if I hadn't rolled onto my back, how one floorboard pairs perfectly with its neighbor, touching my tongue this time to the front door, kicking off like an Olympic swimmer for the final lap, and when I return, it's dark, my wife is asleep, the snail is gone.

Unremarkable

It started with the daily headaches. The oncologist was not too concerned but ordered the brain MRI just in case. The first time I had one twenty years ago I was twice the size and couldn't fit in the donut machine. They sent me elsewhere to a pancake model. This time was fine, I knew what to expect, was not claustrophobic, had no plates in my head, had not worked around metal shavings, weighed 184 pounds. Earplugs in place, large mufflers on either side of my head, they slid me in. With each blast I felt my brain sliced into micro-thin negatives, hundreds of them spewing out in a pile next to my head like newspapers flying off a press. Leaving the facility, I wondered how long I'd have to wait for the results this time. With the last CT scan, it was over thirty-six hours. The tumor hadn't shrunk, the cancer hadn't spread, but the most interesting data listed under reproductive organs said "Unremarkable." I tried to laugh about it, but the other news was too serious. This time the results came back within two hours. Good news, everything was normal. But part of me was sad. I had wanted to hear that my brain was not like everyone else's, that it was remarkable.

Skeleton Weed

The Panhandle of Baker County is threatened by a takeover of rush skeleton weed. The noxious-weed supervisor says, "Rush skeleton weed will eat us for lunch over there if we don't take care of the problem." The supervisor and his wife live in nearby Halfway. She threatens to withhold sex if the weed overtakes her tomatoes and cucumbers. He drinks more beer. They sleep back to back with *What's My Line?* reruns playing throughout the night. The *Hell's Canyon Journal* on the Small-TownPapers.com website doesn't tell me everything, but I know how to read between the lines.

From

The email comes in from my friend saying, "Enjoy your mini vacation—from a number of things." It takes me a while to interpret the word "from." What is it that I'm vacating from? From a constant flow of visitors that mostly makes me happy but also tired; from daily telemarketing phone calls from Marriott Hotels and California Duct Cleaning Services; from junk mail; from sitting around the house all day long, in a rut; from eating the same food every day to quiet my gut; from the rage of the blower Arturo uses to clean the leaves off our yard; from the assault of Abraxane and Gemzar that continue to reduce red and white blood cells in my body; from regular visits to the infusion center for one thing or another; from the bird battles that occur at the feeder; from the responsibilities of parenting an adult; from creating lists like this that try to put everything in order even though it's more about chaos. So I change it up, think about what it is I'm vacating to: to a change of scenery; to waking to the coo of doves; to spending dedicated time writing; to time alone in a villa with my wife; to a morning hot tub with my wife; to breakfast, lunch, and dinner with my wife; to my wife, to my wife, to my wife.

Literati

Using the word *literati* sounds so smug and pretentious. I'm not one, but I often pretend to be, find myself at events late into the evening when I should be at home resting, working on maintaining my red-blood-cell count, doing my own work rather than listening to others. But my town is rife with talent. Every night there is something to do. They flock here because we support them, buy their books, ask them to provide us with a personal autograph, laugh at their jokes, cry at their emotionally-laden passages. I won't stop anytime soon. I need them as much as they need me. I need to know that my town is infested with literati. Locusts whose serotonin levels cause them to breed abundantly, to become gregarious and nomadic, feeding on our lush vegetation, on our doting. This plague I invite.

Paul

This world I'm creating needs to be populated by people. Sometimes I'll use code, because I don't want them to be recognized or embarrassed, or because they wouldn't want to be identified. But Paul stands out. He's a taut thread that weaves a strand of burgundy throughout my thoughts. Without him, I'm the same. With him I am wildly different. If we sit and talk for two hours, I fight to keep up, feel my brain cells changing colors with each new topic. When I read his email, I hear his brain cells changing between each word, an inventive, experimental way of viewing and mapping the world. Paul swims. A trail of fingers rippling the water, inviting me in.

Orchid

The orchids plunging from their vase over the counter in the infusion room are beyond gorgeous. If it weren't for the sweet odor that overcomes the antiseptics and swabs, I might think they were carved, sculpted by artists for use in wax museums, accoutrements to accompany the dead rather than the living. "They look fake," a nurse says. "They'll probably last longer than us," I say. I adjust myself in my chair, plant my neuropathic feet on the linoleum tiles, spread far enough apart to increase my balance, unplug my IV stand and pump, and approach the dripping vines, cup a flower in my hands, feel the fleeting pulse in its snipped existence. I rub the purple ink of a petal, expecting residue lodged in the grooves of my fingerprint, but nothing. Maybe we're all fake. Participants in some sick God's experimental lab. I feel for my own fleeting pulse, rub the pale skin of my arm, hoping to leave a mark, something that identifies me as still being alive.

Water Bowl

For over ten years I have driven by a house on Thurber Lane on the way to and from home. I often see a man a little older than me working on projects in his front yard. Sitting on the sidewalk near his curb is a one-quart clear glass bowl full of what I assume is water. For a millisecond, each time I pass, I wonder about the bowl and the water and the intentions of the man, and when I turn the corner, it's gone. Until yesterday, when I slowed, pulled up to the curb, stuck my head out the window. From my closer vantage point, I saw that the bowl was sitting on top of a concrete water-meter lid. That changed everything. I had thought it might have been about measuring and tracking the temperature of the water throughout the day, or capturing vitamin D for tomorrow's coffee, or simply gaining the attention of passing strangers, if for a millisecond. But no. This was about the water company. About the man's anger with customer service. About a peace offering to the water gods. About making a difference in a world where so little is understood and so much is out of our control. I nodded, rolled up my window, happy to have figured something out today. As I prepared to enter traffic, I saw a woman walking her dog stop at the bowl. The dog lapped up the water, and they were on their way. I looked at my eyes in the rearview mirror, cocked my head. Oh, that.

Pedicure

My resistance to getting a pedicure is more of a gender issue than I would like to admit. Not unlike the recommendation by my primary physician a few years ago who suggested I have a mammogram when I was having chest pain. I thought about being the only male in a lobby full of women who had real reasons for being there. I imagined myself in their shoes, in their brains, seeing a man invade another domain where he didn't belong. I ignored his advice.

My fungal toenails offer me a similar dilemma. Because of the diabetes, every twelve weeks I see a foot doctor who trims and buffs them, addresses only the symptoms, never suggests a cure. A friend told me I should go to a nail salon, where they would treat me with a mixture of white vinegar and mouthwash. How about some eye of newt and hair of a sterile rabbit, I thought? I ignored her advice.

Now, with chemo, my nails have hardened, grown long, and neuropathy has crept into my toes and balls of my feet. I'm afraid of the foot doctor because he often nicks my skin and I worry about my risk of infection. I remember hearing stories from my wife and granddaughters about their mani-pedis, the foot massage and soaking, and I wonder if they could help me, if the massage could work some life back into my toes, if their magic could cure the fungus.

But that lobby, and the chairs full of women. What would they think of the single man in the room? Would they be snickering, pointing, or wondering what shade he'd pick? Do they have a private room, a back entrance? Could I get the first or last appointment of the day?

When I think about the possibility of losing my toes, I imagine the mouthwash and white vinegar not only clearing up the yellow toenails but washing away gender, focusing on the task, leaving tradition at the curb.

Janie

Janie or Jane or Jane Ann. She shows up here because she demands it, deserves it, takes her seat in the front row, knows when and how to inhabit appropriate spaces. She says, "I can't imagine a planet without you on it," which makes us both cry. For forty years we have grown with different iterations of ourselves. She as mother, wife, teacher, mentor, friend, hospice worker, grandparent. And now, as a cherished passenger and companion on this new journey. She has been here before me. Double mastectomy and every other imaginable ailment that goes along with a weakened immune system. She does it with humor, with pizzazz, with relentless pursuit. I can't imagine a planet without either of us on it, but we both know it's coming, and try not to fuss about it too much.

Waiting

Even the act of sitting in front of the computer with fingers perched on keyboard, expecting neurons to fire, words to appear. Minutes, hours, a lifetime. Duration matters. In the morning, wide awake, back flat in bed at 4:44, waiting 16 minutes before rising at 5:00. Why wait? This time it's a choice. This time 16 minutes provides opportunity for productive procrastination. Usually it's forced. At the dentist's office, skimming through month-old copies of *Sports Illustrated* and *People.* Someone else's mouth taking precedence over yours. This time the minutes spent are not productive, increase blood pressure. Unscheduled appointments at the DMV. Bring a book. For a timer to go off so you can sprinkle salt and pepper on poached eggs, salivating. In traffic, gridlocked, some place to be, tapping thumbs on steering wheel, trying to calm yourself by listening to K-MZRT, but it doesn't help. For Social Security and Medicare to kick in. For brain MRI and CT-scan test results. To learn your oncologist's name. Sitting in lobbies. For the pharmacists to prepare your chemo drugs. For the nurses to inject you. For the machine to beep letting you know you're done for the day. For next week's session. For James Holzhauer to continue setting records on *Jeopardy.* To learn if there is any shrinkage in the tumor. For a new poem to emerge. For visitors to show up. To read an excerpt from my story "Sweet Jesus." To see our granddaughter graduate from USF. To discover if I will live beyond the 14-month end point suggested by the Stanford surgeon. Waiting to slip out of the waiting mode. Get on with it.

Play

Nobody had writing at the playwriting group last night. So we talked, about the gloom and doom of our country, the world, the people in it, the likely future facing us. As the nose of the plane was about to crash into fiery explosion, Deborah pulled us up, said, "I like to think we need more play." So we played with words, with ideas, talked about Bananagrams and Scrabble and Words with Friends and Pinochle and poker and blackjack. About croquet and tennis, and golf and the Giants and Warriors, and *Jeopardy* and *Wheel of Fortune*, and comedy shows and improv and going to the theater, and getting down on the ground with young children to stack blocks and make snowmen, and strumming guitars and pounding on xylophones. About running barefoot through sprinklers and hanging ten on surfboards and water slides and sliding down grassy hills on cardboard. About erector sets and Hoopla and chess. About three-cushion billiards and bocci ball and Hula-Hoops. About Clue and Code Names and the prizes in Cracker Jacks. About everything we'd ever played or might play. And it worked. We felt better for a few minutes.

Wired

It's not the first waterfall we seek or even the second, but they're along the way. The slow pathway up Highway 1 through Davenport and New Town brings us to Swanton Road, and finally to a private gate with Keep Out signs posted. We know to ignore them, push through, stop at the stone house built in the 1800s and autograph the tattered journal, so someone knows we made it in and out. Depending on the season, Big Creek is gentle or roars. During winter we don boots, stay out of the water, stick to trails. In summer, we fly straight through the middle of the creek, driven like salmon, passing Bill Everson's house on the left, his meditative meadow on the right, race our way to the fallen redwood at the base of the first falls. We rest, replenish with cold water and granola bars, stare up at the 100-foot cascade, ready ourselves for the vertical ascent of the falls that drops us out on top. For the next 75 yards we hurtle ourselves forward, first one there stripping naked and sliding down the smooth granite of the second falls into a shallow pool, not feeling the gashes to our skin. But we're not done. Now dressed, we forge on, knowing what we seek is near. The 12-foot-tall barbed-wire fence we saw last time that passes straight through the middle of the creek, signs that read "Lockheed" and "Private Property" and "Dangerous!" We were appalled last time, are prepared this time. Is it worth it? Of course not, but we are young and stupid. "Charge!" someone yells, and we do, gloves on hands, wire cutters and saws our weapons of mass destruction.

Take Out

What I know about Mei is that she swims at the gym every morning at 6:00 for two hours. I also know she works at her family's Chinese restaurant every day from at least 11:00 to 9:00. When she enters or leaves the In-Shape facility, I never see her smile or talk. I want to think she's in her 80s, but that may be my optimism. When I order my two containers of vegetarian fried rice to go, she's always at the counter, in charge of takeout and cash. This time after paying her I ask, "How is your swimming going?" She lights up, leans closer to my face, tells me how she used to cough, every day. But now, she is healthy, will live to a hundred, gets oxygen running through her blood. Tells me to get in the water. To swim. To change my life. I feel like her family hasn't talked to her in decades. I feel like she wants to adopt me. I can't refuse.

Sins of the Father

"The poetry bug is a horrible illness," says Gary Young, as he reads fifteen new and selected pieces from his work at a backyard fundraiser. The mockingbird accompanying him agrees, as a wren, as a blackbird, as a cricket, as a frog. The five of them serenade the audience, fill them with stories about lightning and mushrooms and miracles and brothers. Gary looks for the bird, smiles, shakes his head, quotes his wife: "I do not encourage birds." Which I imagine means she doesn't provide red sugar water for hummingbirds, doesn't fill trays and cylinders with seeds, never talks to them as if they're children or friends. The illness requires conversations with birds, even those who mock you, requires writing way too many poems about mushrooms. He tried to discourage their sons from becoming poets, but it was too late. The fatal disease inhabits the family blood. They were encouraged to share everything they saw, heard, every bird that joined and mocked them. There is no cure.

Timepiece

The principal called me in on a Monday, opened last year's yearbook, skipped to the few images with black faces. I pointed to the boy I recognized. When I got home I told my mom his name was Tyrone. "Is he black?" she asked. I didn't think to ask why. What does a 12-year-old know about anything? I had overlooked that fact when I explained how my new birthday watch was stolen, the one Grandpa Harold had given me, shiny brown band, bright face with large numbers, much nicer than my old one. I had worn it to the field near our house, the one that ran along the train tracks, the one he ran along after I handed him my watch. "Wow! That's a cool watch! Can I see it?" Of course he could. I was quiet, shy, in a new school, looking for friends, I thought as I unhooked the band, set it in his outstretched palms. Tuesday morning the principal called me in again. My watch was on his desk. Two new holes had been punched in the band to accommodate a thinner wrist. I held out my wrist, removed the old watch, set it on the desk. "For Tyrone," I said. I'm still not sure.

Color

Certain colors are found hidden at the fringe of nature. I track them in a handmade journal, categorize them. Some are easy. Like the cerulean blues and fiery reds twisted together in angry clouds. They inhabit the beginning pages, easy to find and name. Turquoise mascara encircling the eyes of peacock feathers. The seven colored earths at Chamarel. The yellow and green depths of the Morning Glory Pool at Yellowstone. Other colors are more difficult to access. They occupy the middle of the journal. The glistening red cilia of bloodbelly comb jellies that swim the midwaters of the Monterey Bay Submarine Canyon. The lilac-breasted roller in East Africa. The bubble-gum-pink hue of Lake Hillier in the Recherche Archipelago. Other colors have yet to be found. They inhabit the imagination and blank pages in the back of the journal. A platinum aura around an unnamed planet in an unknown galaxy. The blond wildflower sprouting from the cracks in a dilapidated headstone in an abandoned graveyard somewhere in Iran. A bird residing in un-inhabitable regions of Thailand, its Brandeis head feathers and cerise chest impossible for the naked eye to view. Hunting for something new and better. It's these empty pages where I spend most of my time. Never satisfied.

Maps

There's a guesthouse at Stanford. It's nestled on a hillside at the Stanford Linear Accelerator Center. Google Maps sends you to a gate that requires a badge. We tried those directions twice, found another entrance, gave the guard our name, were pointed in the right direction. The young couple in front of us checking in were asked why they were there. The man said, "We're conducting an experiment." When asked the same question, the wiseass in me wanted to say we were also conducting an experiment. Instead I told the clerk of the 7:30 CT-scan appointment. In my dreams that night, the young man took my place at the scan. They stuck him with an IV, filled his body with iodine, slid him into the machine, took x-rays of his healthy pancreas. I went to the two-mile-long linear accelerator sitting in the middle of 426 acres of pristine surroundings. I stood at one end waiting for the laser to fly down the tunnel and change me. Three Nobel Prizes produced here. What's a little tumor?

A Recipe for Closure

This is how you do it. Make sure you're born to grandparents who have a gorgeous piece of property called Hidden Hill that stretches halfway to paradise, the perfect spot for your memorial. Raise roosters that crow at will. Consciously spend your whole life objecting to war and injustice. Write about it. Talk about it. Care for others more than you do yourself. Spoil your granddaughter as often as you can. Make a living and life building and kindling fires. Say things like "Good business and good humanity are not mutually exclusive." Obsess on baseball, especially the San Francisco Giants. Refuse to go to the hospital one more time. Just before you pass, open your eyes, tell them, "It's a party." When your friends and family speak to the crowd gathered on hay bales in your meadow, inhabit the body of the loudest, brightest rooster. Waddle your way into the circle. Listen to your friends sing "Amazing Grace" and "Here Comes the Sun." Make some noise. Remind us who you were. We remember. We mourn. We celebrate.

Eclectic

We have an eclectic garden. Karen keeps it alive with nasturtiums, salvias, zinnias, and impatiens. The front yard is guarded by our mosaic monkey, on all fours, ready to pounce and spit at intruders. My dad's porcelain seagull rests in an old birdbath. Three miniature maple trees fill the courtyard. A musty typewriter gathers rust and waits to have its keyboard touched again. In the back, the old sewing-machine base holds a glass tabletop, invites us to sit in the sun. A white mixer from the 60s holds rocks and owl pellets. Antique lamps and candleholders light the way to the view. All that's missing is a tuba. I want to bury the base in mulch. Plant thyme and sage in the bell. Blow life into them. The banged-up one I found at the flea market was three hundred dollars. A trumpet would be cheaper. Or a recorder. One seed sprouting from each hole.

Need to Pee

The need to pee has made me a better person. At first it was diabetes. Then chemo. I thank them both, for waking me during lost hours where I usually remember nothing. Now at 2:00 or 3:00 a.m., I have conversations with others, with myself, uncover buried secrets, live futures I never expected, decide what I want for breakfast. Just this morning George appeared, told me again about his trip to Happy Canyon, Utah. How he traversed his way through Poison Spring and Dirty Devil. Found a spot on a nearby ridge to plant lightweight chairs, drink a few beers, watch the devastating thunderstorms around them drench everything and everybody. I've never been. Never really been much of anywhere. I need to mark some new territory. Chicago. I'd like to visit the Art Institute. See the Cornell boxes in person. Pee on trees in Millennium Park.

Uber Options

I've developed a new service for Uber, training drivers to provide therapy. It would work like this. I'd search for Uber Therapist. Let's call him Raj. The fifteen-minute ride to Bookshop Santa Cruz, the perfect amount of time to discuss why I get angry at Verizon customer service. After a healthy role play, he would drop me off downtown and recommend I purchase *The Cow in the Parking Lot*. On a drive to the Nickelodeon, I'll read him a short story, get his critique, and he'll tell me to pay attention to the way the director of *The Souvenir* twists emotion with trust. Eventually I'll book longer trips. Raj will take me to Stanford for a radiology consultation, wait patiently in the parking lot, ask me all the questions a friend would ask. Before we begin the trek from Santa Cruz to Los Angeles, he'll fill the tank, find all the charging stations for his Prius Prime. By the time we reach Staples Pavilion, I will have read him my whole novel, taken notes on his feedback, given him a nice tip.

Digression

My friend and I sit and gab for two hours every week. We pretend to have an agenda. We email each other items to add to the list. Next week we'll talk about her trip to Denmark and Germany, about castles and trains. The upcoming Tony Awards. The new tariff on Mexico. And while neither of us ever says, "But I digress," we both do. One segue leads to another, we go sideways and snake around. We willingly jump down rabbit holes, always find our way out, sometimes with a question: "Where was I going with this?" The other will answer, taking it back five or six degrees of separation before locating the thread, tugging it, realigning ourselves. Moving forward until the alarm on her phone goes off. Either she has someplace to be or is worried about my energy. "But wait!" I'll say. "We haven't talked about *The Biggest Little Farm* yet." On our feet by the front door we'll continue for another fifteen minutes. Do I feel guilty for her delay? Yes, every time. But I care less and less about guilt.

The Fine Line

Sometimes the fine line thickens, becomes wide enough to live in, where cohabitation is possible. Partners in sync, pursuit of mutual purpose. It's when the line becomes so thin it's almost invisible that trouble begins. "You make me feel helpless," the sick one says. "But I just want to help," the healthy one says. It's here where the line disappears, morphs into a net that ensnares both, gathers them up and binds them in knots. They battle the same deep-sea monster from different angles. One struggles with the head, tries to avoid sharpened teeth from ripping flesh. The other grips the slippery tail, sharp fingernails digging into skin and scales. Eventually they kill it, together, barbecue it, eat it with rice pilaf and roasted corn. They are satisfied for a while, until they see its brothers and cousins circling in the distance, looking for revenge.

Ears

I have known my mom for 68 years. She was the first to see me enter the world bloody and screaming. The first to put a diaper on me. The first to bathe my whole body and keep me healthy. When the second course of chemo worked its magic on my hair and beard last month, I shaved off what was left, went directly to Mom's so she could see the new development. She didn't say anything, just smiled and nodded. When my sister visited her the next day, she was serious, looked Shelly in the eyes, said, "I never knew your brother had such big ears."

Rocket Man

The boy visits Elton, as a tortured youth, while he sets words to music, when he drinks and snorts and carouses, at a failed attempt of normalcy in marriage, as he takes the stage in costumes that mask the pain, during every day of rehab, simply seeking requited love. The father and mother are not able, damaged by circumstance and war-torn lives. The boyfriends are shallow, enamored by the wealth and lifestyle. The fans are fickle, wanting what they want when they want it. Sobriety is the trick. Houdini escaping the water torture cell. Is this another sentimental love poem? Boy meets boy. Men adopt children. I don't think so. Addiction keeps its hands stiff around the throat. Demands self-respect. Forces you to seek out the boy and hug him every day.

Loom

I'm finally conducting surgery on the loom Diana gave us two years ago. It was warped. Didn't work for her anymore. Took up too much space. Like working on a new cadaver, I remove bolts, twist screws, harvest organs made of fine maple to be repurposed, placed in new bodies, projects that will live on. Frames for boxes inspired by Joseph Cornell. They will fill a delivery room, these newborns. Invite a navigation of the imagination. Attract fitting ephemera, old photos and pictures of birds, odds and ends mined from flea markets and thrift stores, unlikely pairings that eventually cling together like magnets. Patience the final ingredient. The thing that petrifies dead trees into stone. If we could only bottle it. Live long enough to use it well. I'm trying. Equal parts of poise and urgency.

Icterus cucullatus

I can obsess on almost anything—decorative paper, the perfect crème brûlée, the works of Alice Munro—but birds have eluded the metal traps of my brain. Not that I don't love them. I can watch them at the feeders on our deck for hours, see the hierarchy unfold as the woodpecker bumps the blue jay. But they slip away, disappear, I lose interest. Until yesterday, at John and Bette's house on Branciforte Drive, where we were introduced to the hooded-oriole nest. Have you seen one? Have you held it in your hands? The oriole as master seamstress stripping palm fibers from a frond, weaving them together in unique pieces of art to birth their young. My obsession has shifted. I may form a nonprofit. I haven't seen an actual bird yet, with its golden mane. Need to buy a pair of Swarovskis, find a location, hide myself, wait. Prepare to teach humans what birds already know.

On and On

On January 4, 1945, the *Askov American* newspaper shared that 80 accidents were reported to the Minnesota Conservation Department during the 1944 hunting season, 63 injuries and 17 deaths. 32 persons were injured or killed by shooting themselves, 28 shot by others. Of the 17 deaths, 9 were accidentally self-inflicted. 27 accidents occurred while shooting pheasants, 23 accidents while hunting ducks, 22 while hunting deer. What is it that the department is trying to conserve?

The Hive

I listen to an unfamiliar voice on the radio. Danusha Laméris talks with him, asks him questions about his writing, his life, his illness. He sounds a little like someone I used to know. A smooth and soft delivery. A confidence rooted in uncertainty. He reads his newfound poetry. Talks about the future as if there is one. Recalls past lives. As a teacher, a student, a Little League baseball player. I want to know more. Want to call in and ask him about chemotherapy. Does it hurt? Can he taste it? Does he compose poems while sitting in the infusion chair? It's when he reads the final poem that a crack appears in the shell, and I realize I already know the answers. Now I want to ask myself a question: Are you wallpapering your tomb with words?

The Hunt

Henrietta is the great blue heron who patrols the large field at the corner of Soquel Drive and Thurber Lane. She took a hiatus when the owners let the grass grow taller than her head. The day after the mowers showed up, she reappeared, strutted to the middle, let us all know she was back. We drive below the speed limit to watch her work. The regal neck stretches upward. The golden beak points. She senses movement at the gopher's hole. Stiffens, moves her head closer, strikes with a vicious thrust. A quick death from the mallet-like stab, the gopher hangs limp from her beak. Henrietta sucks the lunch into her gullet, finds a puddle of water to help wash it down. She catches two more, tosses them aside, hunts for the fourth. Like much of the natural world, she eats for sustenance, kills for pleasure.

What I'll Miss

This is what I'll miss: my wife's hand reaching over in the middle of the night to touch me; the burnt-brown-sugar flavor of homemade butterscotch pudding; the unbridled laughter while watching the genius of improv performers; the view of the bay from the Crow's Nest while eating banana pancakes; admiring Joseph Cornell's boxes; hunting and gathering at antique stores and flea markets; waking early in the morning to write; the smell of barbecued food on neighbors' grills; dimples on the face of Tony and Mandy's daughter, Yara; our grandchildren; driving around Lake Tahoe and stopping at Harvey's for a poker tournament; three-cushion billiards; my sister Shelly's inquisitive mind; my mom's amazing quilts; sinking a forty-foot putt; following a good mystery on PBS; the orange rolls at Silver Spur Restaurant; the mosaic monkey in our front yard; reaching over and touching my wife's hand in the middle of the night; writing and finishing lists like this. I'll add to it tomorrow, and the next day.

Missive

I write letters that I don't send. I hide them in a folder called Unsent Letters. I imagine there will be enough for a book by the time I'm finished. It will be published posthumously. Unless I burn them first. I'd rather my grandchildren not read them. To learn about that side of me. The one where I use a little sarcasm and wit combined with a lot of anger to chop my victim's legs off at the knees. I'm too good at it. It's a secret I'd like to keep. That my thoughts can be hurtful. That I will say something when I see inequity. That if you work in the customer-service department you should be serving your customers. That if I open my heart, there could be blood. And only some of it will be mine.

The River

The Dragon Moon had no windows. Just a glass front door painted black. And the best music in town. My friend Peter the DJ helped me join the club, told everybody I was straight. I played pool. I danced. I sweated through three shirts every night. The best few years of my life. I wasn't looking for sex. Or love. I was looking for acceptance. What better way than hanging with folks who lived their whole lives with unacceptance. Bobby the owner was a former taxidermist. His lover Sugar left with another man. And they closed. It's now a post office. With windows. I don't frequent it. If I did, I'd remember bartenders Larry and Michael stopping every night to delight us with their routine to "Take Me to the River." I'd remember when I still had cartilage in my knees and could dance all night long. I post my letters elsewhere. Dance only in my head.

Clearance

A bluebird lands on our feeder. Neck feathers are sheared, like he's been pulled through a meat grinder. I wonder if he even knows. If he compares himself to others. Watches himself grow old and tattered. I do. On early art projects, I'd use my thumbprint rather than a signature. I want to do so again. When I look at my thumb, I can't tell if my eyes are getting worse, or if I've lost my print. The stamp pad clarifies. Nothing there but smooth skin. This identity theft catches me off guard. Makes me wonder who I am. I worry about passing security clearance if I want to volunteer at my grandson's school. If I commit a crime, how will they book me? I may need to test it. I'd stop short of murder. Maybe aggravated assault. I'll settle for petty larceny. Three peaches and a pair of 1.50 reading glasses. They may laugh at me at the station. But I'll laugh right back when my thumbprint eludes them.

The Threshold

If I could assemble my own chorus, it would look like this: Mary Oliver, walking through her doorway into thanks with prayer; Lydia Davis, saying goodbye to Susie Brown; Amy Hempel, with an entourage of rescued animals; Lynn Nottage, flaunting her intimate apparel; Roberta Flack, singing "strumming his pain with my fingers"; Virginia Woolf, writing in her own room; Georgia O'Keefe, painting flowers and posing as one; Murasaki Shikibu, waiting on herself with *The Tale of Genji*; Josephine Baker, dancing at the Folies Bergère, holding a protest sign; Ruth Bader Ginsburg, fighting for her notoriety; Indira Gandhi, mobilizing Indian women for the cause of independence; Mother Teresa, serving the poor and disadvantaged. Twelve peers, if not by age, at least in spirit. To judge me not. This band of angels, coming for to carry me home.

Vertigo

Whenever a response opens with "I thought you meant," the world skews sideways. The honey on the comb oozes out and makes a mess. Bees pollinate elsewhere. You've said, "Let's take a drive." The other says, "I thought you meant we should take the car into the shop to have the brakes checked before we stop at Gayle's to get some picnic supplies on our way to Big Sur." You pause. Vertigo gyrates you. One of those amusement-park rides where your feet end up above your head. The other's thinking and search for meaning have revised this short history. You want to lash out. Make sense of this chasm. Understand how the brain works. Or doesn't. Instead you say, "Let's take the Honda and stop at Phil's, then head over to Pinnacles to get a good look at the tarantulas and condors." You wait. Watch the face. See the eyelids twitch. The other's mouth opens, about to form a train of words, closes, finally says, "I'll drive." You smile, say, "I'll get the keys."

Pathways

It's happening again. When I type "2017" on my keyboard, it appears as "201." I assume the "7" has taken the same mysterious pathway as half my socks, my fingerprints, and a couple dozen pairs of reading glasses. I like to think the unseen rats in the attic are responsible. For all of it. I visualize their encampment above our heads. My socks as sleeping bags. Glasses as bed frames. How they would use fingerprints and "7s" eludes me. I fear my dad might be involved. Or Don. Don would focus on my language, say "Why 'fear'?" Dad has found his next life as their interior decorator. Debbie could be up there as well, directing ratters' theater productions, which explains the noise. When Joe joins them for morning coffee, takes over recruitment, I begin to understand. Kitty's uncle conducts their orchestra. My uncle Gene leads group therapy sessions. From gas chambers in Germany, to dryers that eat clothes, to the traps I set in the heater closet. Loss encourages loss.

Prey

My friend George and his partner took her grandson to see the wildflowers in Death Valley. They veered off onto a seldom-used road that took them to a wild flurry of colors and flowers just this side of a lone oak tree. Explorers that they are, they walked toward the tree, checking out the desert flora and fauna. George saw it first. Peering into a large burial ground of owl pellets, thousands of little skeletons, femurs and skulls, burning white in the heat, dropped there from above by their predators. A rustle in the leaves of the oak, three long-eared owls emerged, soaring. Within seconds a golden eagle shot from the tree in pursuit. George began a steady but frenzied pace in circles around the oak tree, hunting for the eagle's burial grounds, filled with owl bones and more.

Blake Wilbur Drive

I could find it blindfolded by now. Highway 17 to 280 to Alpine Road to Sand Hill Road to Pasteur Road to Blake Wilbur Drive. Where we valet park for ten dollars. Where I have CT scans and blood draws for the CA-19-9 tests. Where I meet with the surgeon. Where he tells me there's no shrinkage, that vascular complications remain. Where I meet with the radiologist to learn about the Cyberknife radiation procedure, told it could gain me six months to a year. Where on the way out, we stop to admire the collage art of Stanley Grosse hanging on the walls. It's what I remember most about the visits. The vibrancy. Attention to detail. A love of life that leaps from its frame and clings to me. At home, I'm asked about the trip to Stanford. I don't say a word about the upcoming endoscopic procedure to implant gold beads in the tumor. I don't mention the planning sessions where CT scans and PET scans and body molding will be analyzed by physicists. I say nothing about the five days in a row of radiation therapy I'll receive. I forget everything. Except Stanley's art that inhabits my smile, guides my words, wraps my body in a protective seal. Instead I tell them I may be in love, how I can't wait to get back to Blake Wilbur Drive.

Ponder

Sometimes I ponder the miracles of my life: Have I made it all up? The crisp view across the bay that outlines Pacific Grove and Jacks Peak accentuated on the horizon. The French toast at Silver Spur drenched in butter and maple syrup that soothes my stomach. My granddaughters—Georgia's determination and Hannah's love of the pun. How my wife and I joke about the way she hides my things. Fabrication or remembrance. Did I hear that bird thud into the window, or did I read about it? I live on a planet with finite resources. I've stored some of them in my brain, hoarded them for myself. Eventually I'll have trouble distinguishing the found objects from the ones I've created. Is the face I'm now wearing real, or the one I had last year? It doesn't matter. I'll return all of it soon, the fool's gold and 24-carat.

A Week Off

A flight to Hawaii. A stay in Tahoe. A drive to Pismo Beach. A jaunt to Oregon to view the handmade books in the Special Collections Library at Reed College. We've done all of these with our weeks off in the past. We've relaxed on beaches, played poker in casinos, eaten fresh clam chowder, and taken photos of new ways to stitch and bind books. The seven-day respite looks different now. No cars or planes needed. No advance reservations. It's the fourth week of a four-week cycle. Week one there's the blood draw, the follow-up visit with the oncologist, the time with Gemzar and Abraxane in the infusion chair. Week two: repeat. Week three: repeat. Week four: the week off I've come to expect. Freedom from the needle, the poison. A chance to recover. But it never works. I recover nothing. I long for white sands and green felt. Bring me back. Let me go.

Memorial

I love my wife so much. It almost hurts to think about it. Not the twenty-six years of loving marriage. The finding ourselves at a twenty-year reunion at the Cocanut Grove. Not Mr. Dick's chemistry class in 1967. Or the making of books we discovered together a few years ago. Not our glorious grandchildren. It's that unavoidable trifecta that invades my thoughts. The one always looking to organize the world sensibly. The one seeking combinations. You know how it goes: the past informs the present, the present determines the future, the future loops back to the past to avoid mistakes. It spins, a hamster on a wheel. When we pose the question: memorial or no memorial? That's when the ache starts to pound with heartbeats. How can we think and talk about this upcoming event? When I tell her I have my playlist ready, that "Another One Bites the Dust" is first, followed by "When the Music's Over" by the Doors, we don't know whether to laugh or cry and end up with both. If we don't think about a memorial, decide instead that neither of us wants one, maybe it won't be necessary. That's when the ache rages into pain. Of course, it's necessary. Of course, I will not be able to hold your hand and sob with you as the playlist ends with John Prine's "Please Don't Bury Me." Of course, we have to play the trifecta, knowing that either way we lose.

Afterlife

My two uncles are dying. Uncle Gene is 92, living with his extended family in Richland, Washington. He's had the MRSA superbug, pneumonia, a broken hip. His younger brother, Uncle Ken, at 91, is 7,223 miles across the Pacific in Lucknow, India, with his adopted relatives. He has dementia, infarctions on both sides of his brain, and has been unconscious for nearly a month. Their younger brother, my dad, has been gone for thirteen years. If I believed in an afterlife, I'd imagine him, lit Winston in hand, waiting for them, shaking his head, asking, "What took you so long?" If I believed in an afterlife, I might have gone looking for him years ago.

Kathy

How do you rave about someone and maintain a sense of credibility? Not have your gushing be so over the top that folks don't trust your analyses? I've seen it in others and I take two steps back, look sideways at the giver and the receiver. I don't see that I have a choice. It's a risk worth taking, and it's embodied in a collection of praise that is much milder, making it rise above the others. I don't know that Kathy is a well-kept secret, because I think she does for everybody what she does for me. She wields a cyberknife that cuts to the bone, scrapes out calcium deposits, lubricates joints, makes my prose feel more real than it is, makes my plays presentable. She asks "Why?" at every perfect juncture to improve the quality of one's work and ideas. She sits with me in front of a fire, has watched me become the incredible shrinking man, lose all the hair on my body, become someone she wouldn't recognize on the street. We keep a running agenda that never ends and the visits are always too short. She helps me understand how to shrink my ego, how to prepare for the disappearance of bravado, how to accept the disappearance of my body, my soul, my spirit, my poems, and eventually the use of the word *my*. Because she knows me so well, she will be able to manage my ultimate disappearance better than the rest. Maybe.

Missing

My grandpa Wes operated heavy equipment in the 60s to knock down trees to carve a highway through Northern California. One fell sideways and crushed his arm, which was later amputated above the elbow. For the rest of his life, he swore he could feel an itch on the hand no longer there. Sometimes I'll run a brush across my scalp through missing hair. Will you roll over in bed in the middle of the night and reach to cuddle a body that's no longer there?

Karen

I'm not sure if Karen's sainthood will be enacted before or after I'm gone. She's a lapsed Catholic so that might have influence on the selection committee. A good pope won't care, will focus on the merits of her case. The biggest hurdle will be that she's still alive, will become the first living saint. While the pope will be looking for two miracles, he will have to wade through her many. She cooks steel-cut oats for me with sliced bananas and walnuts with a separate bowl of brown sugar. She makes me poached eggs on toasted English muffins. She hunts through the fridge to make sure she doesn't feed me anything past the expiration dates. She walks Pepper to the corner three times a day, filling perfumed poop sacks. She doodles in her journal every morning. She listens to more Audible books than anyone on the planet. She waves at every neighbor when we come and go. That I am still alive is her biggest miracle. She has pushed my expiration well beyond its "use by" date.

The Extra Year

The poet Brenda Shaughnessy read at Peace United Church last week. She said that she'd been struggling with writing an opera libretto, but had just been given an extra year to finish it. What would I do if I were given an extra year? The first week I would make a list: (1) travel to Mürren, Switzerland, take a tram into the carless town, eat frog-leg scampi at the restaurant with the view of the Eiger, Mönsch, and Jungfrau; (2) while in Europe, revisit the Rodin Museum, admire *The Gates of Hell*; (3) return to Amsterdam to hunt for the houseboat with more than fifty cats; (4) write a minimum of 365 new prose poems; 5) spend more time watching birds; 6) add items to this list; (7) continue to add more while doing nothing.

Perlino

I ache to confess, but I don't know how or what. I'm not allowed in churches anymore. Confessionals are off-limits. I find an outhouse at a construction site. It's blue, which is perfect. So am I. I step inside and sit, wait for a priest to appear and talk to me through the vent. Eyes closed, I'm flatbacked in my bed, composing words on the ceiling with the sulfur tips of long matchsticks. "Forgive me, father, for I have sinned." Something like that, isn't it? But I have not sinned. And it's the mother I seek. I ignite the flame, etch my thoughts in fire, find a meadow on a hill above the city, surrounded by cream-colored perlino Andalusians who ask to hear my story. I share mine, and they theirs. We absolve each other. They prance away our mutual guilt, fling punishment and obligation from their manes, lay themselves down with me around a bed of coals. Can you see this, Mother? Do you feel their heat? Forgive me, please, this race I'm winning. Don't worry. I have the horses. They will bring me home.

~ ~ ~

Acknowledgements

- "Capture and Release" was first published in *82 Review*, Issue 7.2, in print and online.
- "Smooth Dirt" was first published in *82 Review*, Issue 7.2, in print and online.
- " Burn, Baby, Burn" will appear in the next issue of *Chicago Quarterly Review*.
- " Missing" will appear in the next issue of *Chicago Quarterly Review*.
- "'P' Club" will appear in the next issue of *Chicago Quarterly Review*.
- "Almost Done" will appear in the October 2019 issue of *The Sun*
- "Lather" will appear in the October 2019 issue of *The Sun*
- "The Extra Year" will appear in the October 2019 issue of *The Sun*
- "Port" will appear in the October 2019 issue of *The Sun*
- "Role Model" will appear in the October 2019 issue of *The Sun*

So many people to acknowledge and thank:

- Elizabeth McKenzie for unrelenting support over the years as friend, mentor, and editor.
- Danusha Laméris, for her wonderful guidance, deep poetic knowledge, and insights into what works and doesn't work.
- Ellen Bass, Joe Stroud, and Gary Young, who along with Danusha Laméris, wrote me extraordinary blurbs for the book, and all of whom have been muses and inspirational to my writing over the years.
- The members of the poetry workshop who critique my work so well every week: Courtney, Dana, Jessica, Katie, Michelle, Nancy, and Paola.
- Kathy Chetkovich, who sits with me every week in front of a

warm fire, has heard me read every poem, gives some of the best feedback on the planet, and works her way through a weekly "agenda" with me. And thanks to her for editing the complete manuscript.

- Thanks to Jon Silver and Jon Franzen and Cheryl Brothers and Karen Ackland and George Merilatt and Julia Chiapella and Joni Perry and Ed Anderson and Scott Ellis and John Moir and Karen Conley and Paul Skenazy and Clifford Henderson and Kitty and Bob Dixon and Michelle and Dana Massie and Jeanne and David Rosen Sofen and John and Flo Mizelle and Dave Culver and John Sandidge and Melinda Erickson and Neil Joeck and Diana Rothman and Susan Forrest and Alison Gold and Chuck and Alison Parham, for sitting with me in front of the fire and sharing stories about our lives.
- Jennifer Sweeney, poet and manuscript consultant who has held my hand and helped me make critical decisions about poetry content, titles, order, and more.
- Janie Crabb, a 40-year friend who comes over every week to help us make books, and who has been with me through every step of this new life.
- Thanks to my sister, Shelly, who makes me comfort food like Armenian rice pilaf, tapioca pudding, and potato soup. And to my mom, who has given me 68 years of loving support.
- Thanks to the friends and family of Kit Anderton whose words and thoughts at his memorial helped to craft the poem "A Recipe for Closure."
- Thanks to Jon Silver, http://migrantmedia.com, for the author photo and for the video he produced of me reading poems.
- Thanks to Irene Reti Photography, https://ireneretiphotography.smugmug.com/, for the cover photo.

And to Karen, Jeannie, Ali, Hannah, Georgia, and Pepper, who make my life worth living.

OTHER ANAPHORA LITERARY PRESS TITLES

*The History of British and
American Author-Publishers*
By: Anna Faktorovich

Notes for Further Research
By: Molly Kirschner

*The Encyclopedic Philosophy of
Michel Serres*
By: Keith Moser

The Visit
By: Michael G. Casey

How to Be Happy
By: C. J. Jos

A Dying Breed
By: Scott Duff

Love in the Cretaceous
By: Howard W. Robertson

The Second of Seven
By: Jeremie Guy

CPSIA information can be obtained
at www.ICGtesting.com
Printed in the USA
FSHW010446200919

9 781681 145082